The abilities in me Foundation

www.theabilitiesinme.com
Registered Charity No: 1197965

Published in association with Bear With Us Productions

© 2022 Gemma Keir
The Feelings in Me - Anxiety
www.theabilitiesinme.com

The right of Gemma Keir as the author of this work has been asserted by her in accordance with the Copyright Designs and Patents Act 1988. All rights reserved, including the right of reproduction in whole or part in any form.

Paperback ISBN: 9798398554694
Hardback ISBN: 97818046740

Edited by Emma Lusty and Claire Bunyan
Illustrated by Eve Morgan

www.justbearwithus.com

The feelings in me
Anxiety

Written by Gemma Keir

Illustrated by Eve Morgan

I want to tell you a story about this feeling **inside of me**. It's something that you may not notice, and it is called **anxiety**.

ANXiety

It can make me feel **overwhelmed,**

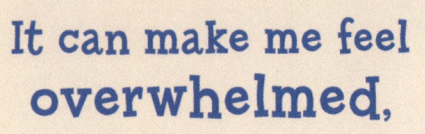

and my tummy may **flip around.**

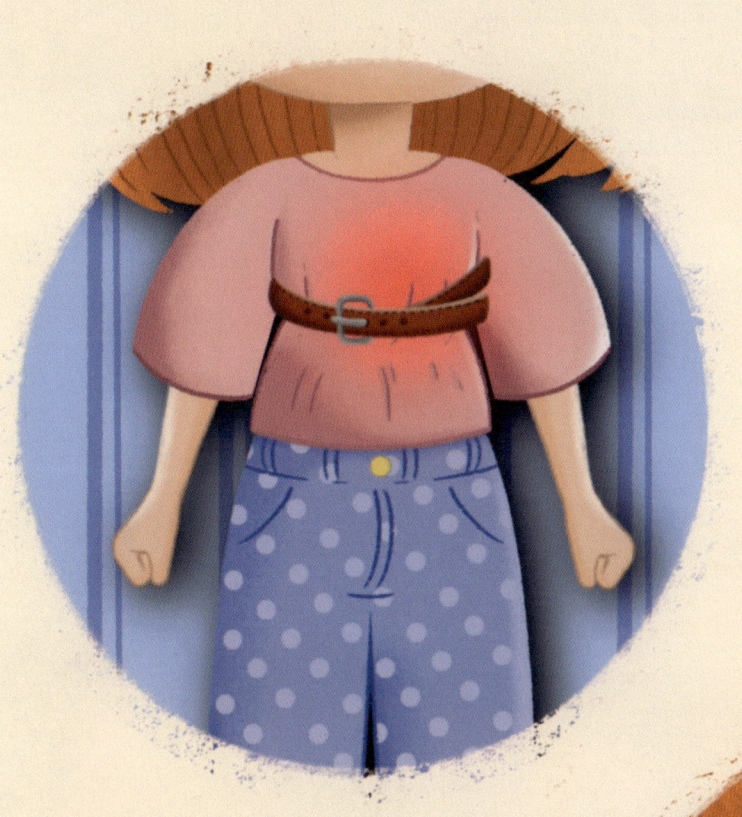

I can feel my chest **go tight**

as I struggle to **hear sound.**

It happens when I feel worried, scared or fearful inside.

It makes me feel a **rush of emotions**,
and I want to **run** and **hide**.

I can feel anxious about **going to school,** or sometimes to **an event.**

The idea of being around people makes me feel closed up and tense.

It also happens when I'm at home,
if I **overthink** the 'what-ifs' too!

These worries become overwhelming, and my thoughts I believe to be true.

My body begins to panic,
as my symptoms start to appear.

Then I **worry** about those symptoms, get **lost** and **feel** the fear.

My thoughts don't always **make sense**;
so many **rush** through my head.

?

Sometimes I need to take myself to **curl up** in my bed.

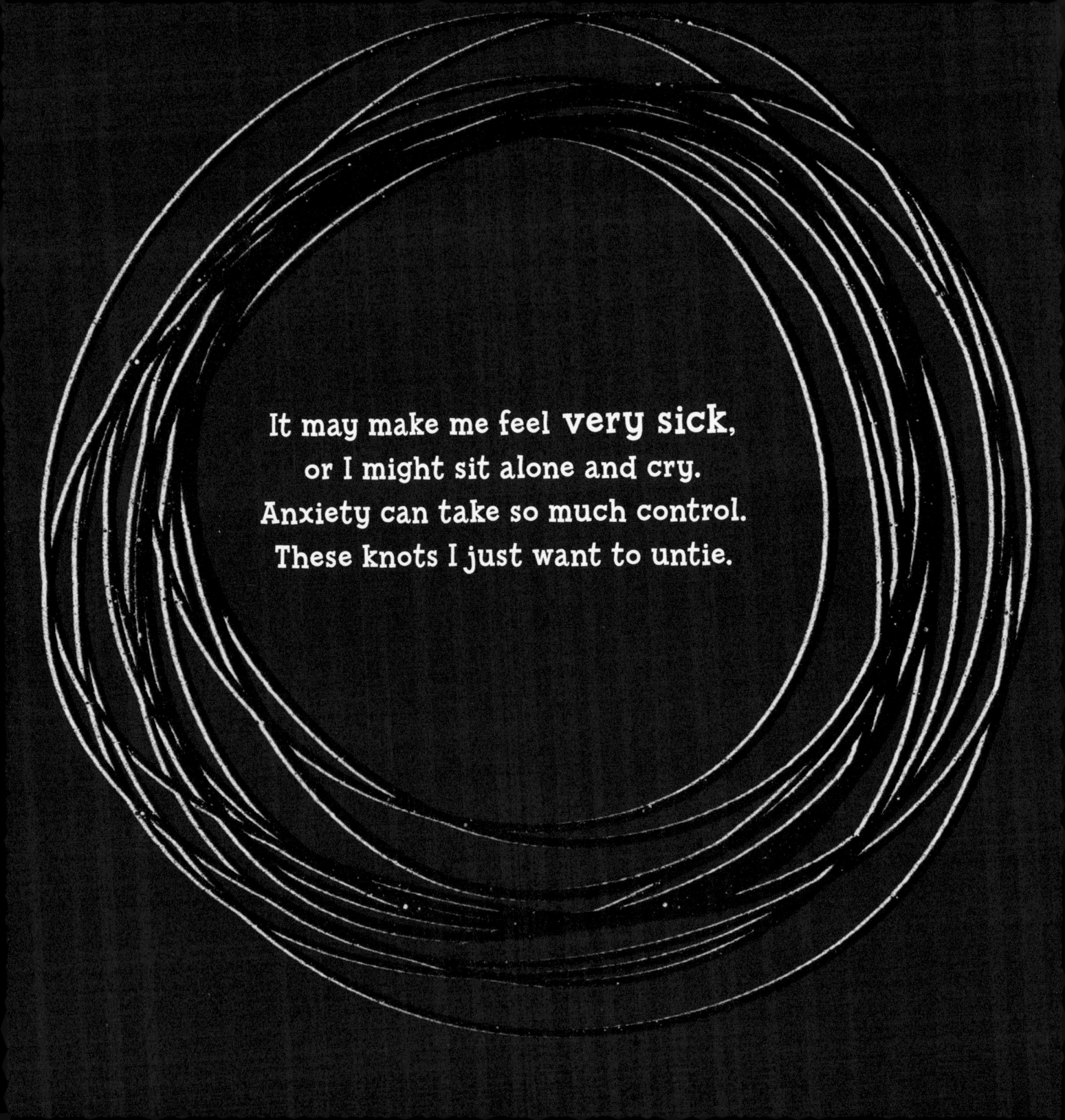

It may make me feel **very sick**,
or I might sit alone and cry.
Anxiety can take so much control.
These knots I just want to untie.

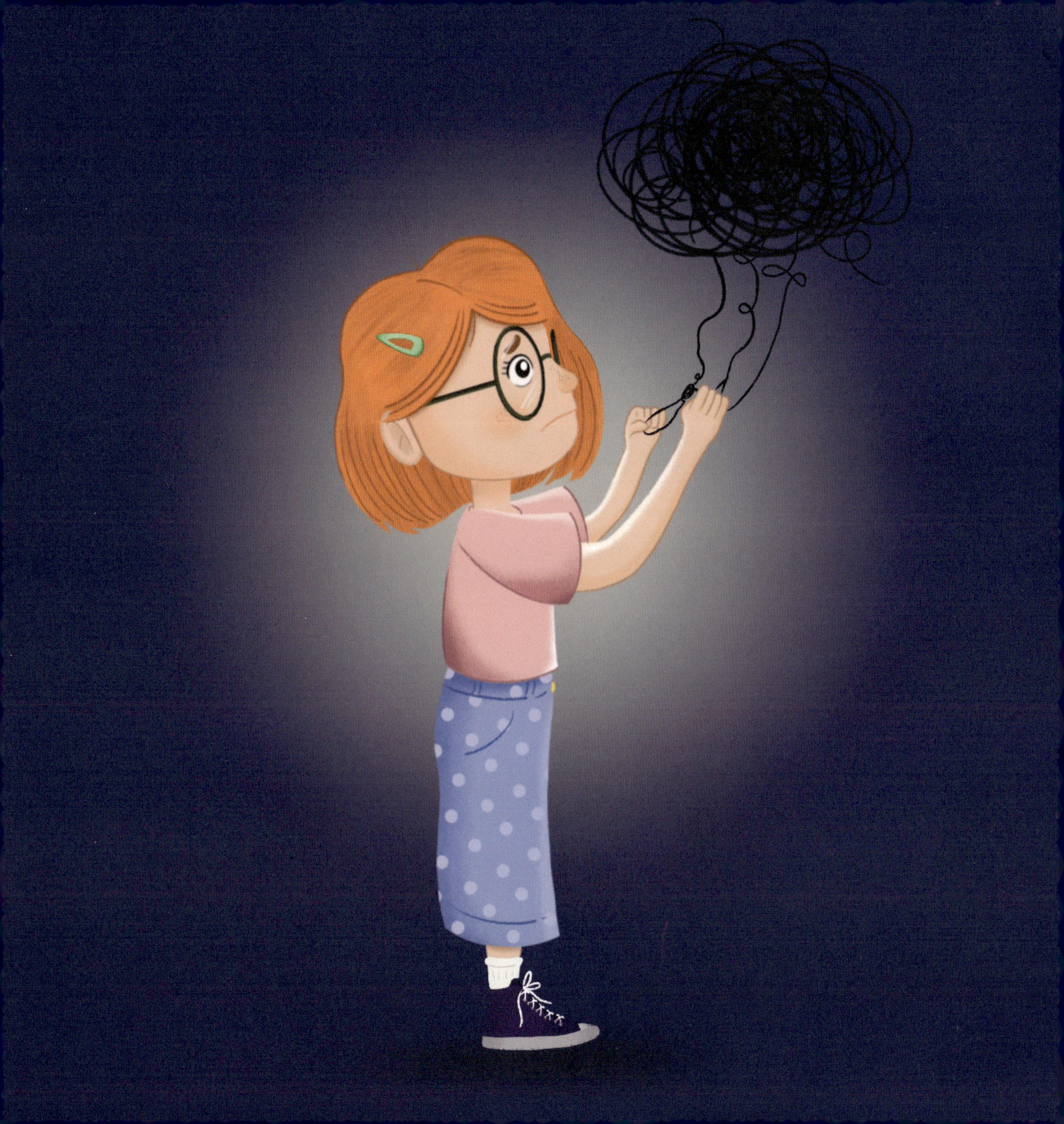

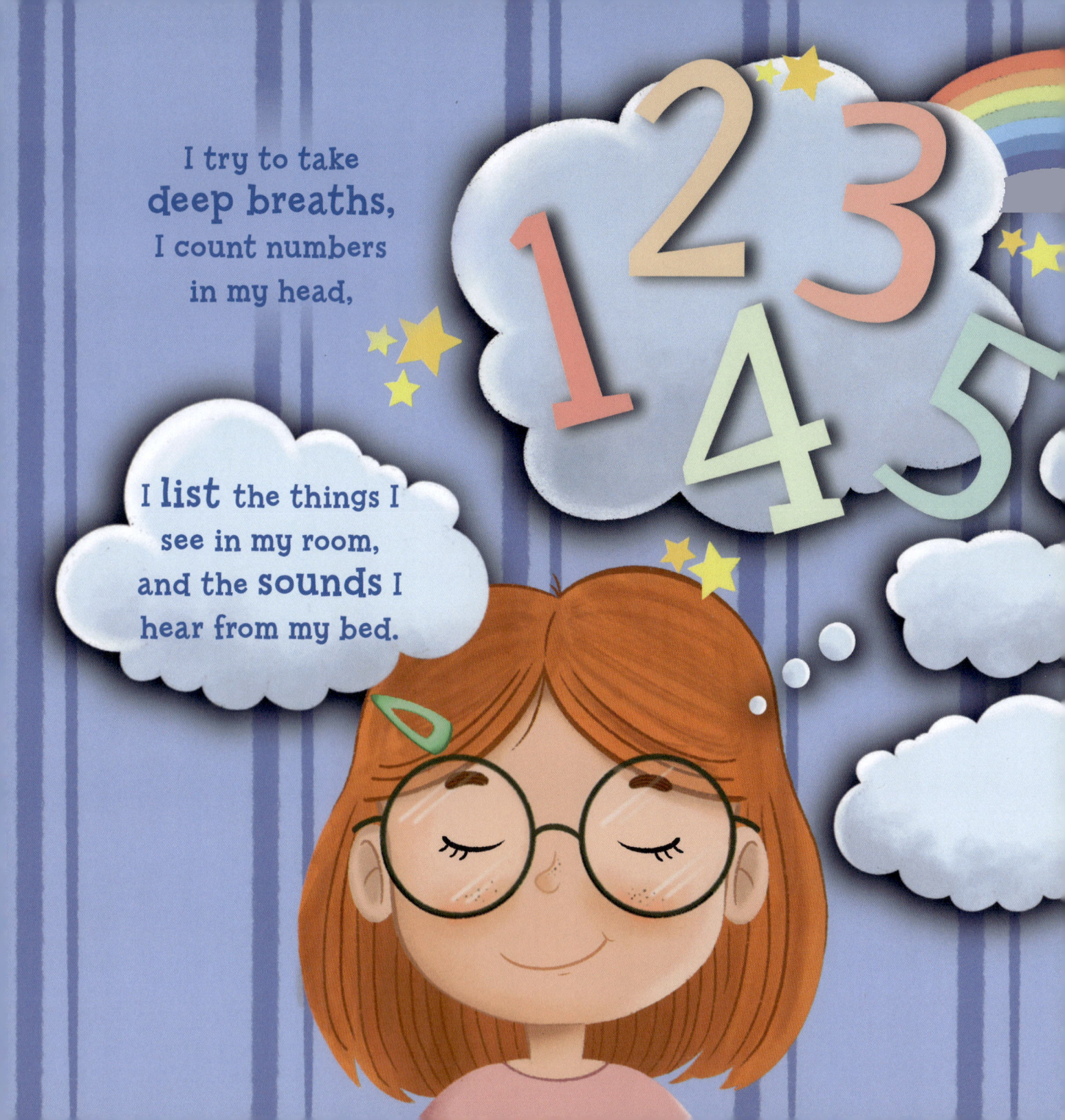

I try to take **deep breaths**, I count numbers in my head,

I **list** the things I see in my room, and the **sounds** I hear from my bed.

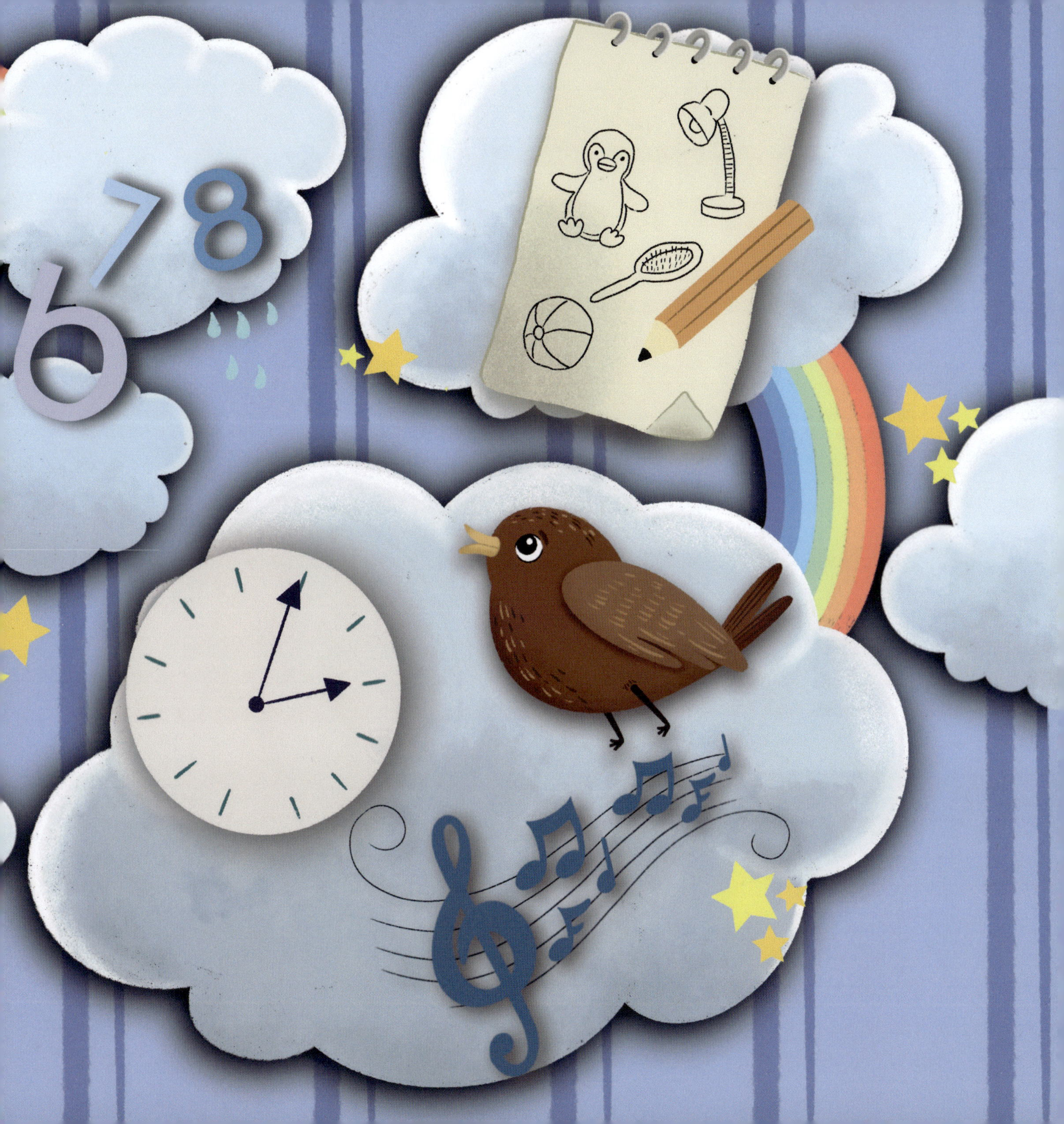
678

It's important that we **speak** to someone
if we feel anxious inside.
It is part of our emotions
and **we shouldn't** let them hide.

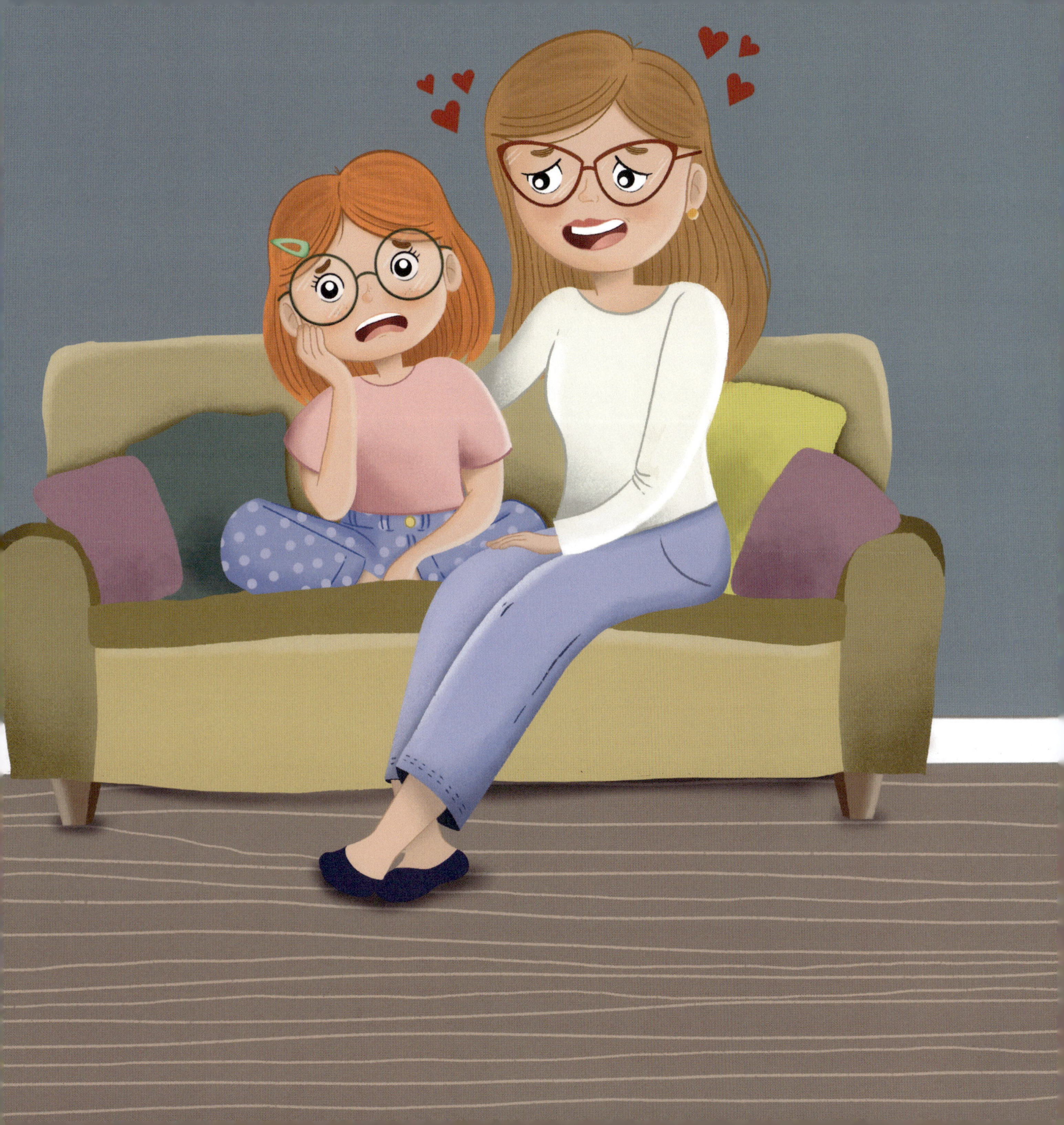

It's okay to talk about your worries,
it's important that you do -
someone could be there to help
and understand what you're going through.

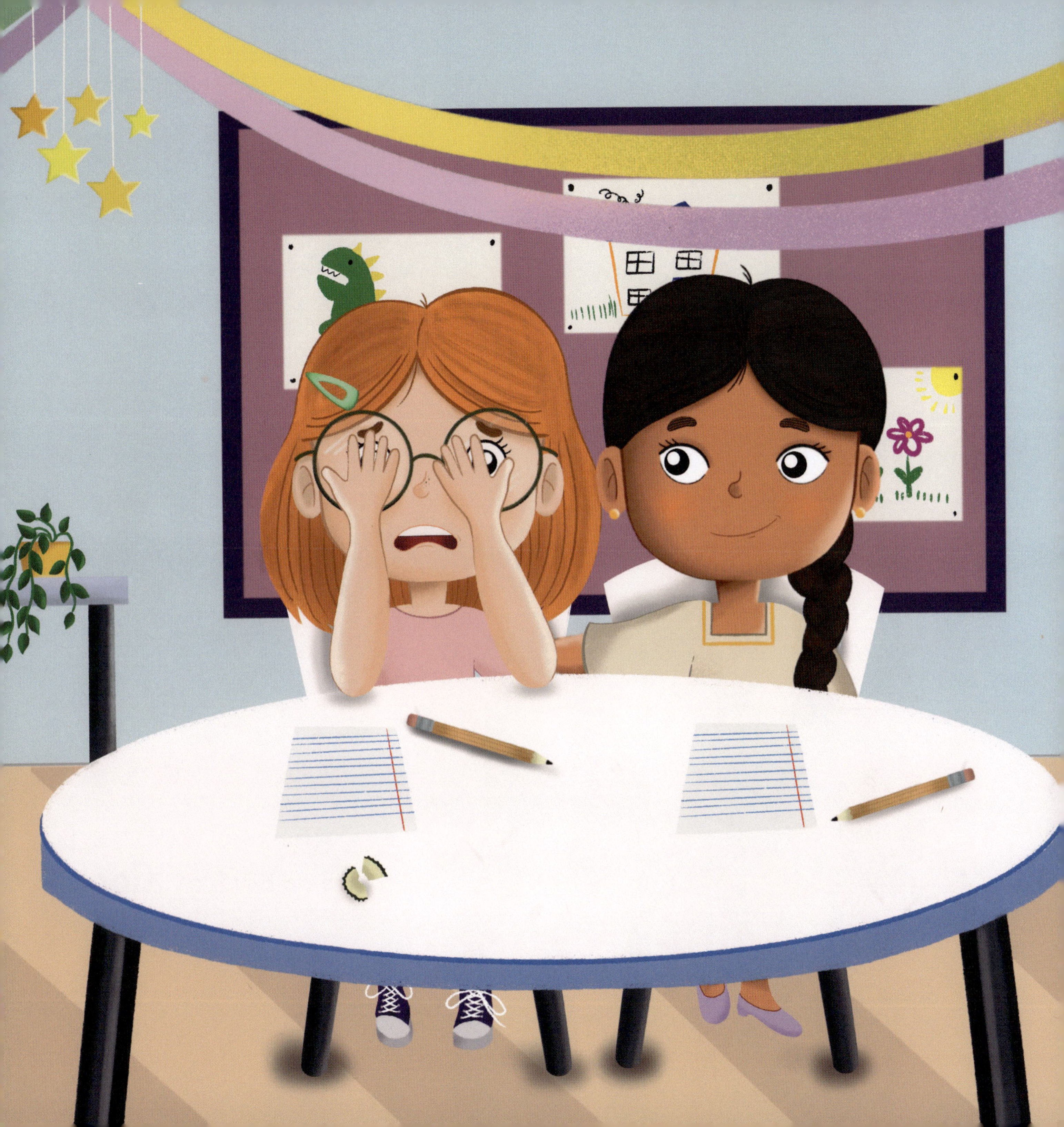

Lots of people suffer with anxiety,

who feel **worried**, **scared** or **alone**,

so it's important we reach out to our friends,

and our family in our home.

Take a deep breath and be mindful and breathe along with me.

Just know that you are not alone - together we can beat anxiety.

ANXIETY AFFIRMATION

I can breathe!

I am Loved! So, so LOVED!

It's okay to talk about my feelings.

My voice MATTERS!

YOU GOT THIS! I am brave. I am strong.

The feelings in me

@theabilitiesinmefoundation

@egm_illustrations

The Feelings in me

The Feelings in Me is a mini series which is a spin-off from the popular **The Abilities in Me collection.** Written by children's author Gemma Keir, this series is primarily aimed at a young audience with bright and colourful illustrations and provides invaluable insight to help support children in learning to understand and accept their emotions and feelings.

The Abilities in Me Foundation

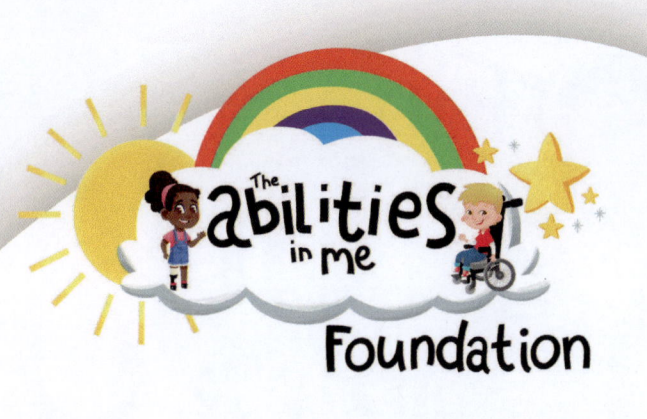

The Abilities in Me Foundation aims to raise awareness of special educational needs and conditions that children may encounter. We have an ever-growing book series written for young people that celebrates what these children can do, rather than what they cannot do. The Foundation also provides community support through forums and special events and works with schools to deliver educational workshops.

At the Abilities in Me, we want all children, regardless of their barriers to feel accepted and understood. The books are inspired by real children and experiences and they enable parents and teachers to talk about different needs and conditions with their children in a fun, safe and engaging way.

Our book series has had such a positive impact on children around the world and we will continue to widen our range and encourage further research and funding into different conditions. The Abilities in Me Foundation aims to raise funds to support worthy causes and by bringing awareness into schools, we hope that this will encourage kindness and reduce bullying.

Registered Charity No: 1197965

Find out more information via our website **www.theabilitiesinme.com**

@theabilitiesinmebookseries

Check out our bookshelf!

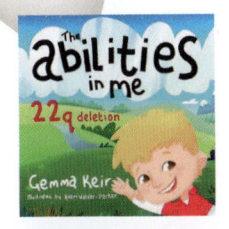

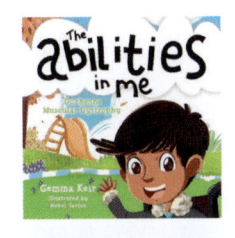

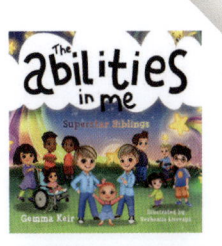

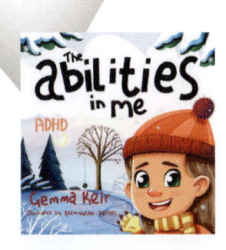

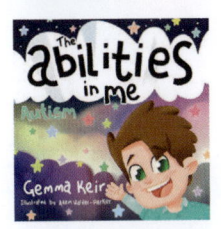

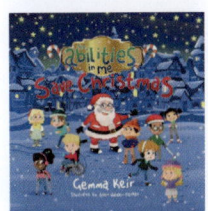

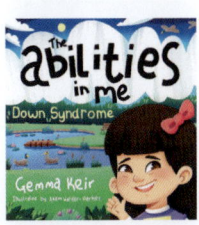

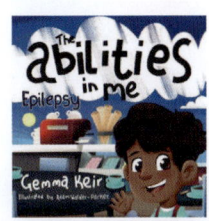

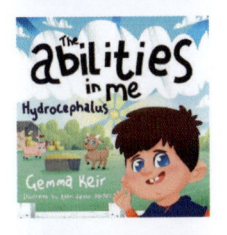

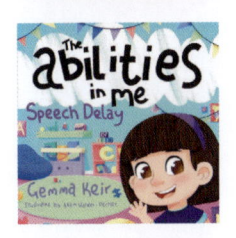

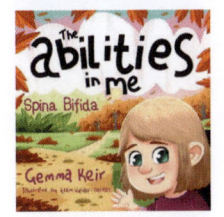

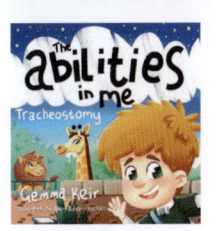

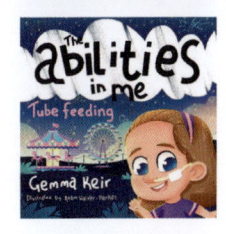

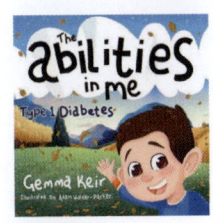

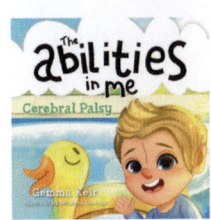

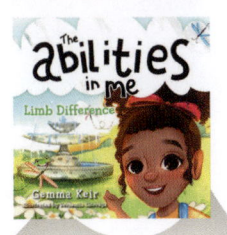

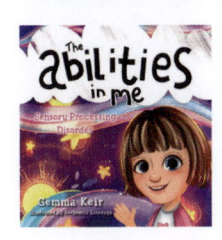

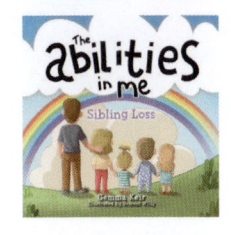

The abilities in me book series by Gemma Keir:

- 22q deletion
- Dravet Syndrome Muscular Epilepsy
- Juvenile Idiopathic Arthritis
- Superstar Siblings
- ADHD
- Autism
- Congenital Heart Defect
- Save Christmas
- Down Syndrome
- Epilepsy
- Hydrocephalus
- Speech Delay
- Spina Bifida
- Tracheostomy
- Tube Feeding
- Type 1 Diabetes
- Cerebral Palsy
- Limb Differences
- Sensory Processing Disorder
- Sibling Loss

Bear With Us Productions

available at amazon

Printed in Great Britain
by Amazon